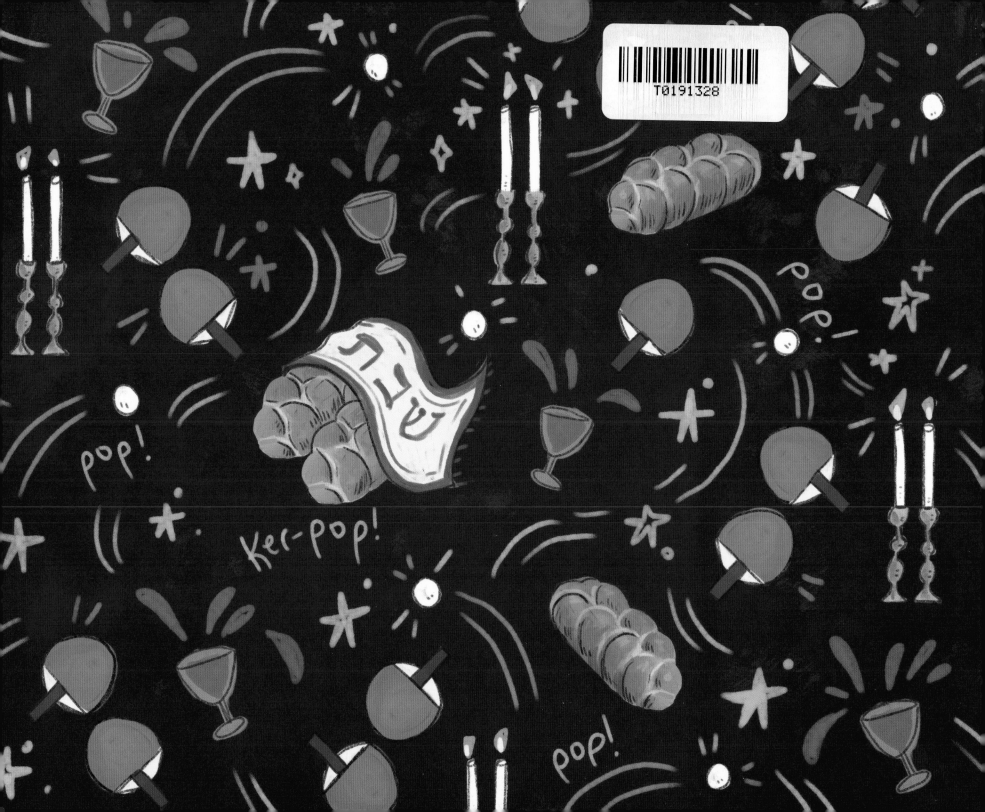

With love and gratitude to Mark, my *gibor chayil* —ADK

To Mom and Dad, for all our lovely Shabbat nights —AR

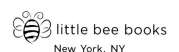

little bee books

New York, NY

Text copyright © 2024 by Ann Diament Koffsky | Illustrations copyright © 2024 by Abigail Rajunov
Designed by Steph Stilwell | Back matter photo courtesy of Estee Ackerman
Manufactured in China RRD 0524 | First Edition
1 3 5 7 9 10 8 6 4 2
Library of Congress Cataloging-in-Publication Data is available upon request.
ISBN 978-1-4998-1609-9 (hardcover) | ISBN 978-1-4998-1610-5 (ebook)

littlebeebooks.com

For information about special discounts on bulk purchases,
please contact Little Bee Books at sales@littlebeebooks.com.

MIX
Paper | Supporting
responsible forestry
FSC
www.fsc.org
FSC® C144853

PING-PONG SHABBAT

THE TRUE STORY OF CHAMPION ESTEE ACKERMAN

WORDS BY **ANN DIAMENT KOFFSKY**

PICTURES BY **ABIGAIL RAJUNOV**

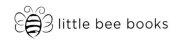 little bee books

Estee watched the ball whiz back and forth between her dad and her big brother, Akiva.

Dad to Akiva.
Akiva to Dad.
It looked like fun.

"Ok, Estee," laughed Akiva, and he gently served her the ball.
Estee swung and . . .

From then on, Estee was in love with Ping-Pong.
For her, it wasn't just a game.
Ping-Pong was exhilarating.
When she played, her heart beat faster.
Her breaths came quicker.
She felt strong.

She practiced and practiced,
and got better and better.
She started to regularly
beat Akiva.

Then one day, she finally beat Dad!

"I think you're ready to sign up for tournaments so you can win against people besides me and Akiva," he said.

"Yes!" she cheered.

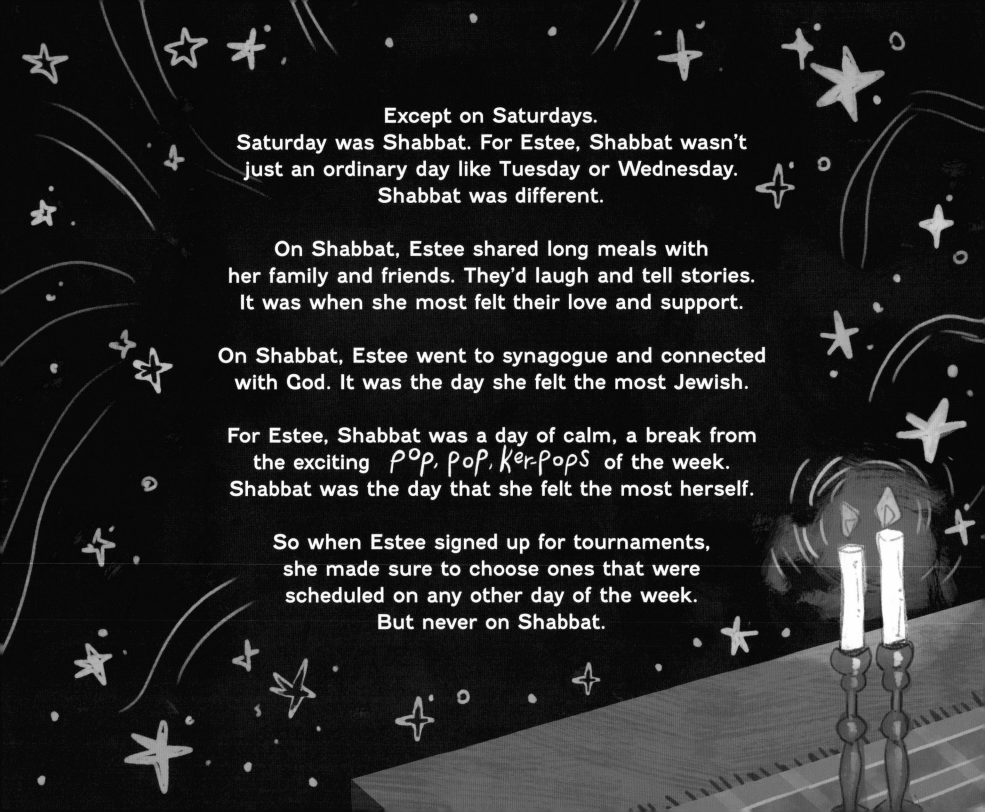

Except on Saturdays.
Saturday was Shabbat. For Estee, Shabbat wasn't
just an ordinary day like Tuesday or Wednesday.
Shabbat was different.

On Shabbat, Estee shared long meals with
her family and friends. They'd laugh and tell stories.
It was when she most felt their love and support.

On Shabbat, Estee went to synagogue and connected
with God. It was the day she felt the most Jewish.

For Estee, Shabbat was a day of calm, a break from
the exciting *pop, pop, ker-pops* of the week.
Shabbat was the day that she felt the most herself.

So when Estee signed up for tournaments,
she made sure to choose ones that were
scheduled on any other day of the week.
But never on Shabbat.

Estee won. A lot.

Tournament after tournament, Estee kept winning.
She beat all sorts of players.
Some were older. Some were younger.
She even beat tennis star Rafael Nadal!

She became one of the best Ping-Pong players in the
United States. She was so good that she qualified
for the most important tournament in the country:
The US National Table Tennis Championships.

At Nationals, each person played many games over many days.
If Estee could beat everyone she played against, she would win a gold medal!

Estee played a
10-year-old named Ivy.

And won.

She played a 52-year-old
named John.

And won.

Finally, Estee played a 16-year-old boy named Dylan.
She looked across the table and served the ball.
Dylan shot it right back. *Uh-oh*, thought Estee. *He's really good.*

First, Dylan was winning.

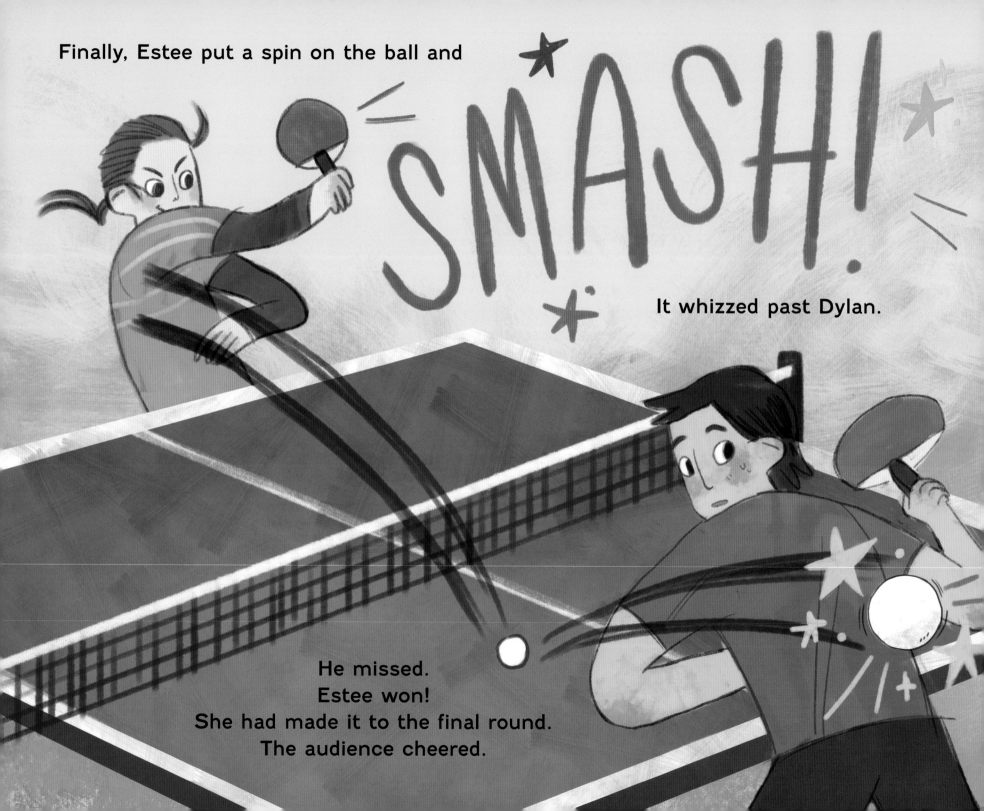

Finally, Estee put a spin on the ball and

SMASH!

It whizzed past Dylan.

He missed.
Estee won!
She had made it to the final round.
The audience cheered.

Estee shook Dylan's hand and ran to her family.
"I'm so proud of you!" her dad said as he swung her around.
"Mazel tov!" yelled her mom and Akiva.

"Congratulations," the officials said to Estee.
"Here is the time for your next game."

Estee looked at the paper.
"Oh no!" she cried.
"It's on Shabbat! Could you please
move the game?" she asked.
"I don't play on Shabbat."

But their answer was NO.
They never moved games.
Not even for Shabbat.

Estee looked at her mom, dad, and Akiva.
"What should I do?" she whispered.
"It's up to you, Estee," they answered.

Estee thought hard.
Shabbat or Ping-Pong?
Ping-Pong or Shabbat?

Pop, Pop... Ker-pop?

Estee knew gold medal chances
didn't come every day . . .

But playing in a tournament
on even one Shabbat felt like
giving up a piece of herself.

Estee made up her mind.

Estee told the people in charge that she would not play.
Dylan, the boy she had beaten earlier, would take her place.

POP!

While Dylan played, Estee sat at the Shabbat table with her family.
She was sad she had missed the chance at a gold medal.
But she knew she had made the choice that was right for her.

The next day, a reporter called Estee and asked her about her decision.
His article appeared later that week.

More followed. People everywhere read the articles. Most of them didn't play Ping-Pong. A lot of them weren't Jewish. But many of them were excited to hear about a young girl who had chosen her values over the gold medal. They sent her lots of letters.

The Time an 11-Year-Old Took Down Nadal

11-YEAR-OLD TABLE TENNIS PHENOM

Talk About 'Heart' Young Table-Tennis Star's a Model Player

To them, Estee was a hero.

The next year, Estee went back to the US Nationals.
After winning game after game,
she again made the finals.

This time, it was scheduled on a Monday.

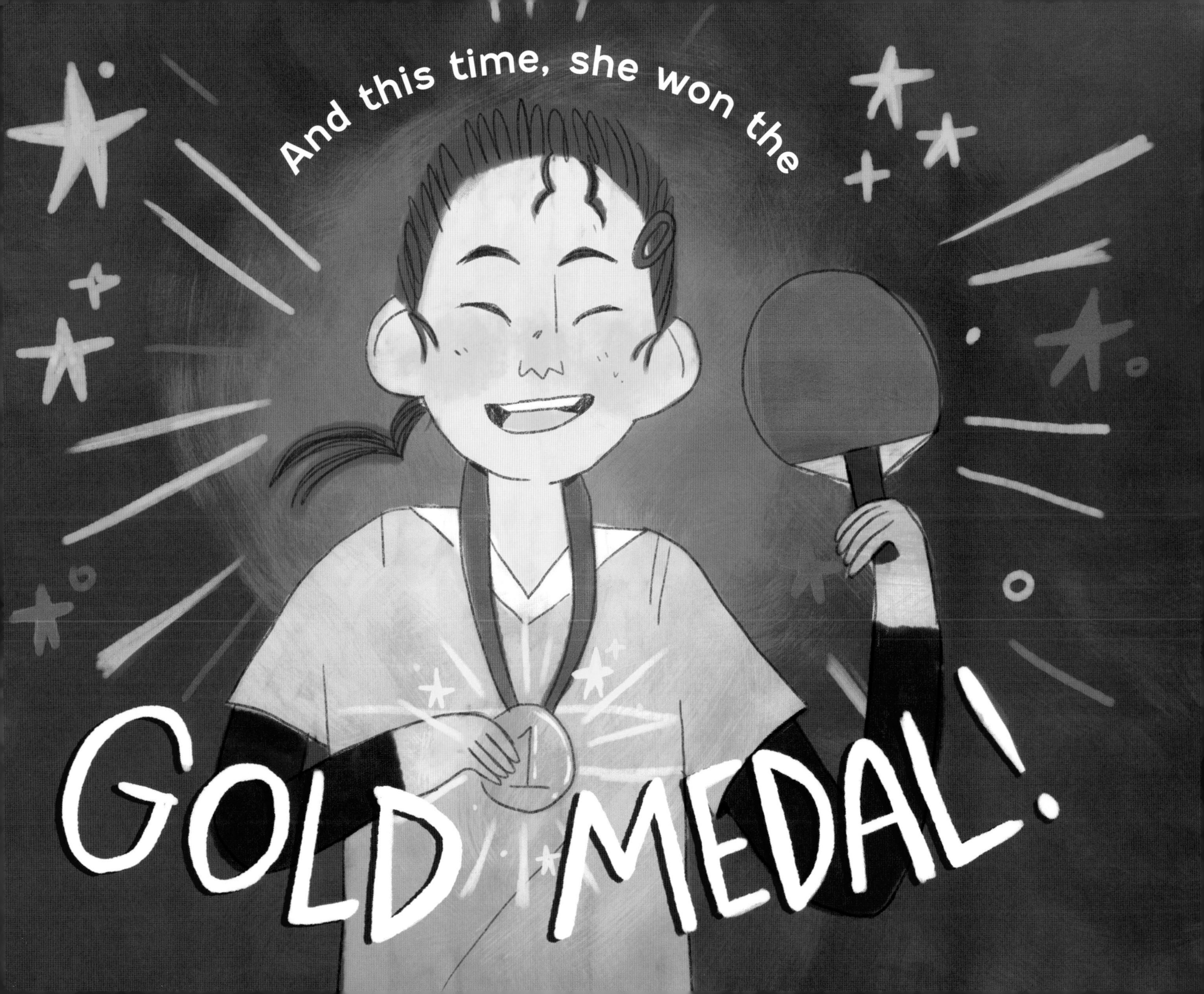
And this time, she won the
GOLD MEDAL!

WHAT'S ESTEE UP TO NOW?

Estee is currently a student at Yeshiva University in New York City. She competes in college table tennis and plans to compete for a slot on the US Olympic Table Tennis team.

Estee is often asked about the time when she chose Shabbat over Ping-Pong when she was just 11 years old, and she loves to share her story. She continues to celebrate Shabbat every week with her family and is grateful that her choice has helped others find the courage to choose what matters to them too.

IN ESTEE'S OWN WORDS:

"The experiences that I have been through have taught me that Judaism will always be my number one priority. Shabbos is truly the holiest day of the week to me and a huge blessing. I hope you learn from my story to never give up your values and shoot for the stars! Dream big!"